THE UNATTAINABLE LOTUS

Badia Kashgari

THE UNATTAINABLE LOTUS

A BILINGUAL EDITION

Saqi Books

British Library Cataloguing-in-Publication Data
A catalogue record for this book is available from the
British Library

ISBN 0 86356 362 7 (pb)

© Badia Kashgari, 2001

This edition first published 2001

Saqi Books
26 Westbourne Grove
London W2 5RH
www.saqibooks.com

To my uncle, Dr Kassem Nour

*The seeds of your love always
blossom in my heart.*

Acknowledgements

My sincere thanks and gratitude to Dr James Steele for his suggestions and comments on my translation of the poems in this book.

Originally written in Arabic, the poems were selected from my three previously published anthologies: *When the Sand Blossoms, Journey of the Soul and Time* and *Some of my Rites*.

B. D. K.

'A man must have chaos in his soul
in order to give birth
to a dancing star.'

Friedrich Nietzsche

Contents

Introduction

One of my first encounters with Saudi Arabian poetry came recently on a visit to Ottawa in the form of Badia Kashgari. Truly surprised and sincerely delighted at the presence of a female Saudi poet, given the renowned paternalism of her country's view of women, the phenomenon of her being a poet at all would have been enough to leave a lasting impression upon me. How wonderful, then, to discover, as well, that not only was she a poet, she was a very true and accomplished poet. Given how difficult it is to sustain for long in any culture the fire of lyrical poetry, I could not help but wonder, what obstacles undoubtedly had to be overcome in order for her to achieve, as she has, both as woman and artist, though one hesitates to distinguish the two, the quality and body of work she has managed to date.

These are the poems of a strong and sensual soul, suffused everywhere with the rich spiritual light of the Arab-Islamic culture she not only inherits as an influence, but furthers, as a living tradition, through her own work and person. Somewhat reminiscent of the spiritual-sensual of the Song of Solomon in the Bible, but not derivative, Badia Kashgari's poetry mingles in its own way, the spiritual-universal and the mundane-specific. To quote Blake, like any true poet, she detects the universal in the specific, sees the universe in the grain of sand and is able through the musical weaving of simple, but ageless symbols, to articulate both. Flame, bird, lightning, sand, rose, night, moon, wave, dawn, heart and God, her poetry orbits like a moth around these eternal candles of the human experience, each one, and more, ignited in her work, by the passion that flows from the heart of a genuine love poet. In poem after poem, Badia Kashgari is either expressing her love, not only of the world and God, but of the particular human face as well, or longing for the exquisite wine and passion of *Laila and her Majnun*, that encounter with the other that releases both like birds into the dawn of union and ecstatic oblivion, that almost Sufic annihilation of one soul in the other. Her poetry does not try to solve the mystery of time and life, but relives in it, celebrates it, and turns with gratitude toward God. Perhaps her Islamic faith has provided her with the confidence to accept life on its own terms, bypassing the despair and confusion that so often plague the kind of poetry that degenerates into merely clever dialectical inquisitions into the meaning of life. With Kashgari, it is different. She celebrates not the meaning of life, but the life of meaning, whether sad or joyous. She is sure of the meaning; she had her faith, but it is the manifestation and transformation of the meaning in herself and in the world that is the true ground of her poetry. How God gets around, shows himself, and disappears around a distant corner playfully beneath everything, even in the exaltation of love, that is her subject. And because she is a living poet practising the living word, her faith and her sense of the living mystery of love and life are not expressed as the usual party platitudes and blind orthodoxies of the dead law and the dead word that lie like bones and molars in the grave.

Rhythmically, too, her work is unique insomuch as English not being her native tongue, but Arabic, she bends her lines like rays of light entering a different kind of water, into patterns and constructions that would not occur naturally to a writer born into the English language. The compositive elements of her poetry reflect an Arabic sensibility in English dress, lending the work a freshness and originality of phrasing that enhance and extend the potential of the English without violating its syntactical integrity. This felicity might be attributed to the happy accident of any genuine poet taking up another language other than that into which they were born, but what cannot be considered in any way an accident is the power and achievement of this poet's solitary, transcendent voice. Though she avows rebellion in poems about Adam and Eve, and to her mother: 'I will never betray my rebellious spirit, or my aspiring voice, for a time yet to come,' Badia Kashgari's work, everywhere, is a sure sign of her creative victory both as an artist and as a woman. Both English and Arabic have been enriched thereby. And for those of us who love and understand poetry, respect and gratitude are the only response.

Patrick White
Poet Laureate, publisher and editor of Anthon's Books
Ottawa, Canada

Between Two Points

From a speck of light, I came into being

There, was the origin of the tongue.

A haven for love,

An olive branch and a flock of doves were also there.

Yet, a bird I was

At every dawn new questions arising within her.

The utterances of the light humming my tunes,

Invigorated by the flame of my spirit.

I, on the verge of doubting altered my course,

To extricate myself from the sins of the blood,

To tread into the labyrinths of my madness.

Little did I know then

That ageless light has long disappeared.

بَيْنَ نُقْطَتَيْنِ

مِنْ نُقْطَةِ ضَوْءٍ نادَيْتُ

هَكَذا، كانَتْ بِـدايات الكَلامْ

كانَ في الأرْضِ مَفازَةُ عِشْقٍ

غُصْنُ زَيْتونٍ وَأَسْرابُ حَمامْ

غَيْرَ أنِّي كُنْتُ طَيْراً

كُلُّ فَجْرٍ يَنْبُتُ التَّسْآلُ في جانِحَيْهِ

كانَ حَرْفُ الضَّوْءِ يَعْزِفُ شَدْوي

يُشعِّلُهُ هَديرُ العُنْفُوانْ

مِنْ نُقْطَةِ شَكٍّ عُدْتُ

أَخْرُجُ مِنْ أوْزارِ دَمي

كَيْ أَدْخُلَ في أَرْوِقَةِ جُنوني

لَمْ أكُ أعْلَمُ

أنَّ الضَّوْءَ أحْقابٌ تَوارَتْ

Was my vision blurred!

Or have the stars abducted me!

And lifted me alone

between my soul and its illusions?

Watch my wings:

Fluttering in a dive,

And their journey, retreating towards the beginning.

My soul seeks tenderness from the depth of words

Alas, how I vanish from the veneer of the earth!

And how my spears break at the cliff!

While being wrapped by dunes of oblivion.

The universe beseeches me to step into its space,

To cast aside my sorrows,

And to deliver my days from what is impossible.

**

قاصِرَةٌ في الرُّؤْيا!

أَمْ هِيَ الأَمْداءُ غابَتْ بي!

ثُمَّ عادَتْ فَتَاءَتْ٢٥

بَيْنَ روحي وَظُنوني.

هِيَ ذي أَجْنِحَتي

تَتَراقَصُ في مُنْحَدَرٍ

تُسافِرُ في ارْتِدادٍ نُحوَ "المُبْتَدا"

تَصْطَفي التَّحْنانَ مِنْ شَجَرِ الكَلامْ

غَثاءُ الأَرْضِ يُقْصيني

وَرِماحي تَتَهاوى في دَرَكٍ

تَتَلَبَّسُني تِلالُ النَّسْيانْ

يَسْأَلُني كَوْني أَنْ أَدْخُلَ دَوْرَتَهُ

أَنْ أَتَخَلَّصَ مِنْ شَجَني

مِنْ أَنْفاسٍ ثَقُلَتْ بِعَصيِّ الأَيَّامْ

***

15

Oh, you perplexing vision!

Return thy captive light to my sight.

Let me

sip the wine of your first tree.

Take me back

to the flock that witnessed my beginning.

And sing my name in the midst of the action,

Like grains growing in the distances.

Transform me into an heroic poem

dwelling in the stillness of the night

And in the remote memory of home.

Rabat, October 1996

يا تِلْكَ الرُّؤيا!

أعيدي الضَّوْءَ المَأسورَ لِعَيْني

دَعيني

أرْشُفُ مِنْ خَمْرَةِ سِدْرَتِكِ الأولى

أعيديني

لِسِرْبٍ يَشْهَدُ فاتِحَتي

وبِصَدْرِ المَشْهَدِ غَنِّيني

سُنْبُلَةً تَخْرُجُ مِنْ ألْفِ مَدَىً

مَلْحَمَةً تَسْكُنُ في أقْصى العَتَماتِ

وأَقْصى ذاكِرَةٍ للأوْطانْ

الرباط، تشرين الأول/اكتوبر ١٩٩٦

17

Memory of a Dream

Waiting still,

At the crossroad of my life,

While my anchor erodes away the days unlike the others.

I reject the moments that are ticked away,

By the pendulum of time.

Would your voice someday return to me!

Would tears prevail over the clouds of my veins!

*∗∗

ذاكِرَةُ الحُلْمِ

واقِفَةً ما زِلْتُ

عَلى مُفْتَرَقِ العُمْرِ

ومَرْساتي تَنْزِفُ يَوْماً لا كَالأَيّامْ

رافِضَةً كَنْتُ لأَرْقامٍ

تُسْقِطُها السّاعاتُ عَلى زَمَني

تُرى هَل يَأْتيني صَوْتُكَ يَوْماً!

هَلْ يَفْتَرِشُ الدَّمْعُ سَحابَ دَمي؟

***

Anchoring my pulse

I returned to the nightwoods

And to the sand flowers.

Infused with the formation of rivers.

I search . . .

In the lexicon of the beginning

and in the scriptures of poetry.

The splashed foam forms your waves,

The scattered leaves in your fields,

Blend in me like the neighing of estrangement.

But like a defiant mare,

I jump over the fence.

* * *

مُشَرَّعَةَ الأنْفاسِ

أنا عُدْتُ

لأشْجارِ اللّيْلِ

وزَهْرِ الرَّمْلِ

أبْحَثُ في قاموسِ البِدْءِ

وقاموسِ الفِعْلِ

وسِفْرِ الأشْعارِ

تَنْداحُ شَظايا مَوْجِكَ

أوْراقُ حُقولِكَ

كَصَهيلِ الغُرْبَةِ تَمْزِجُني

مُهْرَةُ قَلْبي تَتَخطَّى الأسْوارْ

* * *

Listen, the wedding's ashes

Converse with my own lightning.

Here, a glimpse of light filters through my soul.

There, the rustling of a husk,

Mighty winds and rain,

I taste their aroma in surrender to earth.

Why should I be pronounced absent by a concealing pronoun?

Whilst through my voice I am always present,

Singing the melody of the Orient,

And setting the time of pulsation.

Ask my stars about my song,

For, I step not out of one circle,

Except to enter into another of love.

***

هُوَ ذا فَحْمُ الأعْراسْ

يُخاطِبُ بَرْقي

هُنا شَيْءٌ مِنْ نورٍ يَنْضَحُ في الأحْشاءْ

هُناكَ حَفيفُ سَنابِلْ

رياحٌ وأَمْطارْ

أَلْثُمَ نَكْهَتَها فَتُسَلِّمُني لِلأرْضِ

لِمَ يَنْعَتُني ضَميرٌ مُسْتَتِرٌ وأنا الحاضِرَةُ

المُتَحَدِّثَةُ بإيقاعِ الشَّرْقِ

وَميقاتِ النَّبْضْ

عَنْ أُغْنِيَتي أَسْأَلُ أَفْلاكي

فأنا لا أَخْرُجُ مِنْ دائِرَةٍ

إلاَّ كَيْ أَدْخُلَ في أُخْرى لِلْعِشْقْ

***

23

This is my memory of a dream:

The resonance of an echo,

It engulfs me in the elements of the unknown.

It allures me like a forbidden fruit,

I approach your face,

Your sword seduces me.

I approach your guards on land

Only to be blocked away by your other guards on the sea.

Is it my memory that is overshadowed by misty clouds!

As a defiant formation,

Clouds surge on the whirling wind,

The horses of rapture precede me,

They advance, engage, retreat and then depart.

Subdued the star of my life becomes.

The echo of first song fades away

And my name erases its form.

But that who looms beyond the borders,

ها هِيَ ذاكِرَةُ الحُلْمِ

كَتَرْجيعِ اللحْنِ تُدَثِّرُني بمياهِ الغَيْبِ

كَفاكِهَةِ السِّدْرِ تُضَمِّخُني

أَدنو مِنْ وَجْهِكَ

يَسْتَدْنيني سَيْفُكَ

أَدنو مِنْ حُرّاسِ البَرِّ

يُجاهِرُني حُرّاسُ البَحْرِ

أذاكِرَتي يَغْشاها غَمامْ

كَجُموحِ التَّكْوينِ

ضَبابٌ يَنْسَلُّ كَثائِرَةِ الرِّيحِ

جيادُ النَّشْوَةِ تِسْبُقُني

تَتَقَدَّمُ تُقْبِلُ تَتَراجَعُ تَرْحَلْ

يَخْفِتُ نَجْمُ الْعُمْرِ

يَــتَوارى صَوْتُ الأُغْنِيَةِ الأُوْلى

يَنْطَفِئُ اسمي

وَهَذا الواقِفُ خَلْفَ حُدودي

And glances into my stillness,

While I declare I'm wrapped in lavender branches,

In palm-trees of my home,

In the heat of the night

Pouring into the sand of passion.

* * *

يُحَدِّقُ في صَمْتي

وَأَنا أُعْلِنُ أَنِّي أَتَلَفَّعُ بِخُزامى الوَرْدِ

بِنَخيلِ بِـــلادي أَتَخَضَّبْ

بَهَجيرِ الليْلِ المُنْسِكَبِ

بِبَيْداءِ الوَجْدْ

***

With trembling steps and bleeding ribs,

Unperturbed, I proceed,

My lost time weeps for me.

It may not keep my promise,

Or may take me away from you,

Or further, may expel me from your shrine,

But I shall return crowned by your anthems,

To announce

That I am searching for your time, My Home.

And the mare of my bereaved heart

Will remain an intrepid mare

Guided by a memory of a dream.

Dhahran, October 1991

مُجَقَلَةُ الْخَطْوِ مُجَرَّحَةُ الأَضْلُعِ ماضِيَةٌ

قَدْ يَبْكِيني الزَّمَنُ الضائِعُ

قَدْ يَكْسِرُ وَعْدي

قَدْ يَبْعِدُني

أَوْ مِنْ مِحْرابِ رِمالِكَ يُخْرِجُني

لَكِنِّي مُتَوَّجَةٌ بِنَشيدِكَ قَدْ عُدْتُ

مُعْلِنَةً أَنِّي

أَبْحَثُ عَنْ زَمَنِكَ يا وَطَني

فَسَتَبْقى مُهْرَةُ قَلْبي المَحْزونِ

تُضاءُ تُضاءُ بِـــذاكِرَةِ الحُلْمِ

الظهران، تشرين الأول/اكتوبر 1991

Angry

Angry,

When you see me,

Fear not my rage.

Allow me to sail into the depths of your eyes,

Let me escape my weariness.

I, when your eyes talk to me,

Know not how my anger leaves me!

Angry,

I may become at times,

Do not deny my raging temper.

Carry it to the banks of tranquillity,

Collect my tear drops,

Decode my pain,

غَضَبى

غَضَبى

حينَ أُطِلُّ عَلَيْكَ

لا تَفْزَعْ مِنْ غَضَبي

دَعْني أُبْحِرُ في عَيْنَيْكَ

دَعْني أَهْرُبُ مِنْ تَعَبي

إنِّي حينَ تُخاطِبُني عَيْناكْ

لا أَعْرِفُ كَيْفَ يُغادِرُني غَضَبي

غَضَبى...

قَدْ أَصِلُ إِلَيْكْ

لا تُنْكِرْ غَضَبي

خُذْهُ إلى ضِفَّةِ نَهْرٍ عَذْبٍ

لَمْلِم دَمعي

اسْتَقْرِئْ وَجَعي

Try to listen to the echoes of my pulse,

When the waves of your hands caress me,

My anger instantly turns into a musk-rose,

Becomes a joyful hymn,

A sad melody,

Dances in chanting ecstasy.

حاولْ أنْ تَتَحَسَّسَ نَبضي

فَأنا حينَ تُهَدهِدُني أمْواجُ يَديْكْ

يَتَحَوَّلُ نِسْريناً غَضَبي

يُصْبِحُ أُنْشودةَ فَرَحٍ

تَرْنيمةَ حُزْنٍ

تَرقُصُ في طَربِ

Glorification

I woke up today

To witness the universe overjoyed

By incantation.

Why! I exclaimed.

What's so special about my day?

The child within responded:

It is my day.

So, let me cry and pray.

In your hands lie the hymns of my time;

Taste the sweetness of their harmony.

And from their clay let my formation be.

While I twitter like a bird;

Don't scold me.

تَسبيحٌ

صَحَوْتُ اليَوْمَ

وَجَدْتُ الكَوْنَ فَيّاضاً

يُغنِّي

سَألْتُ لماذا؟

وَماذا أَدْرَكَ يَوْمي!

فَأَجابَني "الطِّفْلُ" الذي في الحَنايا

وَقالَ: هُوَ يَوْمي

فَدَعيني أَبْكي وَأُصَلِّي

في يَدَيكِ تَرانيمُ وَقْتي

فَاشْربي مِنْ مائِهِ

مِنْ طينهِ شَكِّليني

حينَما أَهْزِجُ كَالعُصفورِ

لا تَنْهَريني

35

Allow the translucent light

To engulf your heart.

Glorified be Thy Name, oh God, I said.

How overwhelming is Thy Omnipresence.

And when I float in Thy Light,

How little my problems become!

Limassol, April 1997

دَعِي النُّورَ الشَّفِيفَ

في قَلْبِكَ يَخْتالُ

قُلْتُ: سُبْحانَكَ رَبِّي

ما أَعْظَمَ شَأْنَكَ

حِينَ يَغْمُرُني فَيْضُ نورِكَ

ما أَهْوَنَ شَأْني.

ليماسول، نيسان/إيريل ١٩٩٧

Intrepid

My feet slipped

Into the darkness of a swamp

Infested by rots.

I sought help from your inhaling lungs

So that I can remove

What has stuck to my tongue,

This memory of moss!

نَجْدَةٌ

تَنْزَلِقُ قَدَمايَ

في مَجاهِلِ مُسْتَنْقَعاتٍ

تَشَبَّعَتْ بِالعفَنِ

فَاسْتَنْجَدْتُ

بِشَهيقِ رِئَتَيْكَ

كَيْ أُزيلَ

ما عَلِقَ بِاللِّسانِ

مِنْ ذاكِرَةِ الطَحالِبْ

Adam and Eve

Did I not come into your life passively!

Or from the zenith of my mind!

Maybe!

Or perhaps from the depths of my madness?

Or to escape from tumultuous rain?

No.

Rather, I came from the serenity of my clouds,

I come to affirm your being.

Do you know what it means to let me also be?

***

بَيْنَ آدَمَ وَحَوَّاءَ

إِنِّي أَتَيْتُكَ لا مِنْ سُكونِكَ أَوْ سُكوني

مِنْ قِمَّةِ عَقْلي!

رُبَّما

أَوْ مِنْ قاعِ جُنوني.

مِنْ طَقْسٍ أَمْطاري!

لا.

بَلْ مِنْ صَحْوِ غُيومي.

أَتَيْتُكَ لأَقولَ: "كُنْ"

فَهَلْ تَعْرِفُ مَعْنَى أَنْ تَقولَ "كوني"!

***

When we met, I had a reason.

You were the tears and the *kuhl* in my eyes,

When you evoked them, the comets burst into green.

I offered you the humanity of my inner female self,

While you cared merely for the Eve in me,

As does a monk his psalms.

Like you, I too at the beginning was.

Nine months in the womb I stayed,

And by labor I was born.

With closed eyes, I too arrived.

Why should one of us be the victim!

***

يَوْمَ أَتَيْتُكَ كانَتْ لي قَضِيَّهْ

وَكُنْتَ أَنْتَ الدَّمْعَ الكُحْلَ في عَيْنَيَّ

تُوقِدُهُ فَتَخْضَرُّ النَّيازِكُ

وَهَبْتُكَ إِنْسانِيَّةَ أُنوثَتي

وَأَنْتَ تَزِفُّ لي حَوَّاءَ بِدْئِكْ

كَتَواشيحِ ناسِكْ

أنا مِثْلُكَ في البَدْءِ كُنْتُ

تِسْعاً حُمِلْتُ

مَخاضاً حُمِلْتُ

إلى دُنْيايَ بِعيْنَيْنِ مُغْمَضَتيْنِ جِئْتُ

لِماذا واحِدٌ مِنَّا يَكونُ الضَّحِيَّهْ!

***

I cared less when we met

What has been said over the centuries.

I revered you as a branch blessed by plenty,

A song of love hummed in the throats.

Feeble and burdened I carried you for nine months.

I enchanted you like seasons and moving waves.

Where is that Adam, like a fabled bird,

Echoing my voice rather than strangling it?

Where is he, the epitome of my secrets,

As I am his?

✳✳✳

حينَ أَتَيْتُكَ لَمْ يَكُنْ يَعْنيني

ما قالَ الرُّواةُ عَلى امْتِداد القُرونْ

تَلَوْتُكَ غُصْنَاً تُبارِكُهُ السَّنابِلْ

تُفَّاحَةَ عِشْقٍ تُرَتِّلُها الحَناجِرْ

وَهْنَاً وَعِبئاً حَمَلْتُكَ تِسْعَاً

حَمَلْتُكَ فَصْلاً ومَوْجاً يُسافِرْ

فَأَيْنَ ابْنُ آدَمَ عُصْفورُ جَوَىً!

يُغَرِّدُ صَوْتي قَبْلَ اجْتِياحِهِ

أَيْنَ ابْنُ آدَمَ في بَوْحيَ سِرٌّ!

وَفي سِرِّيَ بَوْحُ جِراحِهْ!

***

I cared nothing when we met

Whether you or I was the lesser.

I cared even less about Eve's deceit or her weakness.

Nothing shall destroy my omnipresence,

No matter how one refers to me.

My existence is proved by my voice,

And not merely by gendered language.

I came into your life to sing your name like a fresh dawn.

Nothing will dampen my spirits,

Not even a humble dwelling in the harem.

The melody of your voice shall persist in my verse,

An echo that preceded my sighs.

***

يَوْمَ جِئْتُكَ ما كانَ يَعْنيني

أَنْ أَكونَ دونَكَ أَوْ تَكونَ دوني

مَكْرُ حَوَّاءَ أَوْ كَيْدُ ظُنوني

ما كَنْ يُلْغيني

حَذَفوا تاءَ التَّأْنيثِ أَمْ في قَيْدها رَبَطوني

يَنْبَثِقُ حُضوري مِنْ صَوْتي

لا مِنْ أَلِفٍ، "تاءٍ نِسْوِيَّةٍ" أَوْ "نونِ"

لأَنْشُدَكَ صَباحاً عُذْرِيَّاً جِئْتُ

لَنْ يُثْنيني

سَكَنٌ دونيٌّ يُصلَكُ بِأَقْبِيَةِ الحَريمِ

سَيَظَلُّ صَهيلُكَ في قافِيَتي

كَرَجِعِ اللحْنِ يَسْتَبِقُ أَنيني

***

47

You, the dawn of my beginning,

And the core of my conjecture;

When I came to you, I conversed with myself,

And liberated the future from the fetters of yesterdays.

Because you alone are my present and my life to come,

And your eyes my green fields and shining sun,

I crowned my kingdom with openness of your sharing,

So you may be reincarnated as the beginning,

And return to the land of my faith.

In the book of my life, I inscribed your being,

Do you know what it means to let me also be!

Boston – Dhahran, July – August 1988

يا فَجْرَ فاتِحَتي وشِعارَ حَدْسي

الْيَوْمَ جِئْتُكَ كَيْ أُناجي فيكَ نَفْسي

وأُحَرِّرُ الغَدَ المُقْبِلَ مِنْ جَهْلِ أَمْسي

لأنَّكَ أنْتَ "الأنْتَ" يَوْمي وغَدي

وَعَيْناكَ حَقْلي وشَمْسي

بأنْسِ بَوْحِكَ تَوَّجْتُ مَمْلَكَتي

لِتَعودَ كَما كُنْتَ

عَلى أرْضِ يَقيني

عَلى دَفْتَرِ العُمْرِ هَتَفْتُ "كُنْ"

فَهَلْ تَعْرِفُ مَعْنى أنْ تَقولَ "كوني"؟

بوسطن – الظهران، تَموز/يوليو، تَموز/يوليو – آب/أغسطس ١٩٨٨

Trance

The final day in the calendar of my stars;

My consciousness renders me unconscious

I leave the darkness and the nadir of the brain,

Among bleaky flames of madness

Shrouded by waves.

I cross the threshold of a trance.

Like the light, I unfold my wings from my ribs

To nurture in a distant garden, a birth,

And from the rites of a wilderness pervaded by a desolate voice,

The elements of my being take shape.

Unarmed, I call you,

Embroidered by a cascading glow

That dwells in the amber of the soul,

As another form

I dissipate into the void before creation.

غَيْبوبَةٌ

الْيَوْمُ الأخيرُ في تَقْويمِ أَنْجُمي

وَعْيي يُغَيِّبُني

أَخْرُجُ مِنْ ظُلَمِ العَقْلِ وسَمْتِهِ

إلى انْدِلاعِ جُنونٍ يَتَعَقَّرُ باللُّجَّةِ

أَدْخُلُ في غَيْبوبَةٍ قَدْ بَدَأَتْ

أَفْرِدُ أَجْنِحَةَ أَضْلُعي كَضَوْءٍ

أَقْتاتُ مِنْ رَوْضِ اللاميلاد

وَمِنْ طُقوسِ أصْقاعٍ نَطَقَتْ بِغَيْهَبِ الصَّهيلِ

تَتَشَكَّلُ عناصِري

عَزْلاءَ آتيكُمْ

مُوَشَّاةً بانْهِمارِ تَأَجُّجٍ يَرْقُبُ في مَجْمَرَةِ الرُّوحِ

صورَةً أخيرَةً

أغيبُ، أغيبُ إلى ما قَبْلِ الطِّينِ

51

To reincarnate afresh,

Look you in the face, and become one with you,

Free of former weakness

And liberated from my past aberration.

Abu Dhabi, March 5, 1999

أُبْعَثُ مِنْ جَديدٍ

وَجْهاً لِوَجْهٍ مَعَ اكْتِمالي بِكُمْ

دونَ سالِفِ عَجْزٍ

أوْ سابِقِ ضَلالْ.

أبو ظبي، ٥ آذار/مارس ١٩٩٩

On the Banks of the Impossible

My attempts to trace your trail

You twilight-like being, have exhausted me.

You, who exists in my wandering, my travelling and my
    pulses;

I invite you to walk into my life a lover or a stranger.

Let loose the force of the crown embroidered by a vigil of
    divulgence.

Let the night serenade awaken my body

While this purple sips from my veins and flames,

So that from me, beyond the horizon, moons fall,

And fruits approach my zodiacs and stars.

I am the woman who lost the key of history,

while journeying towards you.

I also lost my lyrics and the most precious of my things,

As filtered ink trickles into my words.

عَلى ضِفافِ المُسْتَحيلِ

في اقْتِفائِكَ

أَيُّها الشَّفَقيُّ أَتْعِبِني اغْتِرابي

يا كائِناً يَمْتَدُّ في خَطْوي وَأَسْفاري وَنَبْضي

أَقْبِلْ حَبيباً أوْ غَريبَا

وَاطْلِقْ سُوْرَةَ العَرْشِ المُجَلَّلِ في نِشيْدِ الليْلِ

يوقِظُ بَوْحُهُ جَسَدي

وَهَذا الأُرْجُوانُ يَعُبُّ مِنْ بَرْدي وَمِنْ لَهَبي

حَتّى أُساقِطَ مِنْ غَيْهَبِ الأَفْلاك أقماراً

وَفاكِهَةً لأَبْراجي وَشُهُبي

أَنا امْرَأَةٌ ضَيَّعْتُ مِفْتاحِ التَّواريْخِ

في سَفَري إلَيْكَ

ضَيَّعْتُ قافِيَتي وَعَصِيَّ أَشْيائي

مِنْ سقْسقاتِ الحِبْرِ في لُغَتي

55

I coupled the hoarse resonance of your voice with my
song,
And to the amplitude of your rites at the crossroads of
love,
I trod holy sands,
Then proclaimed my belonging.
Here, we cover the distances that lie between the end of
space
And the beginning of our talk.
On the vicinity of a dream, my ship anchors for awhile,
And for awhile, another sail looms to which I am
attracted,
Only to be surprised by your quenched flame,
And by pouring clouds.
Pity the soul that succumbs to obedient impulses.
Woe to the heart that seeks refuge from you within you,
While long nights roar inside the self.
Woe to the questions that bend behind the echo,
And beyond the endurance of both you and me,
And among the reverberations of darkness.

زاوَجْتُ بُحَّةَ صَوْتِكَ المَحْزونِ تَرْنيماً بِأُغْنِيَتي

وَإِلى رِحابِ طُقوسِكَ، عِنْدَ مُفْتَرَقِ الهَوى

خَبَبْتُ في الرَّمْلِ المُقَدَّس

ثُمَّ أَعْلَنْتُ انْتِمائي

ها نَحْنُ نَجْتازُ المَسافاتِ ما بَيْنَ انْتِهاء المَدى

وَفاتِحَةِ الكَلام

عَلى تُخومِ الحُلْمِ يَغْفو زَوْرَقي حيناً

وَحيناً يُخاتِلُني شِراعٌ أَلوذُ بِـــوَهْجِهِ

يُفاجِئُني انْطِفاؤُكَ ها هُنا

تُفاجِئُي انْسِدالاتُ الغَمامْ

يا وَيْحَ روحٍ تُشَرِّعُ الأَنْفاسَ للنَّبْضِ الخَنوعْ

يا وَيْلَ قَلْبٍ يَحْتَمي بِكَ مِنْكَ

وَاللَّيْلُ يَزْأَرُ عاصِفاً بين الحَنايا وَالضُّلوعْ

يا وَيْلَ أَسْئِلَةٍ تَنْحَني خَلْفَ الصَّدى

ما بَيْنَ طَوَفانِ احْتِمالِكَ وَاحْتِمالي

وَما بَيْنَ ارْتِدادات الظَّلامْ.

You, the ancient declaring of my themes,

Come to me a lover or a stranger.

Shatter this image of fetters

And plant in your bosom a field of perennial wheat or an
oasis of palms.

Conduct your tune on my body,

Be it melodious or tragic,

And beyond the horizons set me free

Surfing sail or a bird

Soaring in the heights so it may give life to the dawn.

Who is he that crowns me in the universe

As the epitome of civilization.

Who makes me become Sheherazade, mistress of all
languages;

My verse the secrets of silence,

Or the poetry of good tidings!

Who is he that explodes my latent rain? —

يا كائنَ البَوْحِ المُعَتَّقِ في تَراجيعي صَهيلا

أَقْبِلَ حَبيْبَاً أَوْ غَريبا

حَطِّم مَرايا القَيْدِ

وَازْرَعْني بِصَدْرِكَ قَمْحَاً أَوْ نَخيلا

اعْزُفْ عَلى جَسَدي

نَحيْبَاً أَوْ هَديلا

وَعَلى مَدارِ الفَلَكِ أطْلِقْني

شِراعَاً مُبْحِرَاً أَوْ طائِرَاً

يَخْتالُ في الآفاقِ كَيْ يَهِبَ الأَصيْلا

مَنْ ذا يُنَصِّبُني عَلى الأكْوانِ

تاجَاً لِمَمْلَكَةِ الحَضارَة

أَكونُ أنا شَهْرَزادَ سَيِّدَةَ اللُّغاتِ

وَتَصيرُ قافِيَتي اكْتِناهَاً لِلسُّكونِ

أوِ البِشارَهْ!

مَنْ ذا يُفَجِّرُ صَحْوِيَ المَطَري!َّ

59

To irrigate the branches for Ishtar!

Who is he that saddles me,

That saddles history with visions!

So that I may arouse my flame even in icy waters,

Covetously and willingly.

You twilight-like being, in my attempts to trace you,

I walked long; my steps are a witness.

I offered my sacrificial self,

And all that I possess,

Yet my vision persisted,

Alluring and urging me to go back to the beginning.

And to hold fast to the very first step.

For the soul in the kingdom of heaven

May reveal the secrets of departure,

And the stars of your steps,

Beyond the memory of the unknown,

لأغصانِ عِشْتارَ

يُسْرِجُني

يُسْرِجُ التَّاريخَ أَسْمائي رؤىً!

فَأُضْرِمُ في جَمْرِ المياهِ تَبَتُّلي

اشْتِهاءً وَاخْتِيارا

في اقْتِفائكَ أَيُّها الشَّفَقي

سِرْتُ، سارَتْ بِيَ خُطايَ

نَحَرْتُ قُرْبانَ عافِيَتي

وَما مَلَكَتْ يدايَ

غَيْرَ أَنَّ رُؤايَ ما بَرِحَتْ

تُخاتِلُني، وَتَقولُ لي لِلْبِدْءِ عودي

وَتَشَبَّثي بِالخُطْوَةِ الأُولى

فَالرُّوحُ في مَلَكوتِ العَرْشِ

قَد تُفْضي بِأَسْرارِ الرَّحيلْ

وَشُموسُ خُطْوِكِ

خَلْفَ ذاكِرَةِ الغُيوبْ

61

Are the shores; the impossible serenity.

Jeddah – Dhahran, February 1996

هِيَ الضِّفافُ، هِيَ الأمانُ المُسْتَحيلْ

جدّة ـ الظهران، شباط/فبراير ١٩٩٦

In Exile

The map of my life,

Framed by your name

Carries me towards the openness of a distant galaxy.

Where to go?

With a pitch-black night in a spell

Where to go?

My face, outside this universe,

A bird trying to ignite the enclosures of stillness.

Where to?

And my present is a pall

Wrapped again in another pall.

Could it be the present that is hidden in our time

And that dictates submissiveness to the vanity of words?

في المَنْفى

خارِطَةُ العُمْرِ

المُؤَطَّرَةُ باسْمِكَ

تَمْضي بي نَحْوَ أَصْقاعِ مَجَرَّةٍ سَحيقَهْ

إلى أَيْنَ اَتَّجِهْ

وَاللَّيْلُ مُوغِلٌ في تَعاويذِهِ!؟

إلى أَيْنَ اَتَّجِهْ!

وَجْهي خارِجَ الكَوْنِ

طائِرٌ يُشْعِلُ مَغاليقَ السُّكونْ

إلى أَيْنْ!

وَالحاضِرُ كَفَنٌ

يَتَدَثَّرُ بِكَفَنْ

أَهُوَ الحاضِرُ المُنْدَرِجُ في زَمَنٍ

يُعَلِّمُكَ "الخُضوعَ" لِتيهِ الكَلامُ!

Or could it be the sly wreckage of an anticipated time?

My wounds gush blood

And my blood is a wave searching for veins,

While I am left between myself and my blood

Demolishing impossible impediments ,

Searching for the concealed truth.

Ottawa, November 21, 1999

أمْ هُوَ الحُطامُ المُراوِغُ في زَمَنٍ مُنْتَظَرْ!؟

إنَّ الجِراحَ تَسيلُ مِنْ دَمي

وَدَمي مَوْجٌ يَبْحَثُ عَنْ شاطِئِهْ

وَأَنا بَيْني وَبَيْنَ دَمي

أَدُكُّ حُصونَ المُحالْ

باحِثَةً عَنْ وَجْهِ الحَقيقَهْ...!

أوتاوا، ٢١ تشرين الثاني/نوفمبر ١٩٩٩

For a Time Yet-to-Come

How often my mother told me:

Daughter, I wish you were a son!

Looking after you exhausted me;

The rebellion resounding in you

Caused me undue embarrassment.

My mother added preachingly:

Cast aside the worries in your life my daughter,

And accept your destiny

In the fortunes of a husband.

Why not be like the rest of us?

Let me rejoice on your wedding day,

And bestow my blessings upon you.

With eyes fighting tears, I responded:

مِنْ أَجْلِ زَمَنٍ آخَرَ

كَمْ مِنْ مَرَّاتٍ قالَتْ أُمِّي

لَيْتَكِ وَلَدٌ كُنْتِ!

تَعِبَتْ عَيْنايَ مِنَ الرَّكْضِ وَراءَكْ

جَلْجَلَةُ الرَّفْضِ بِأجوائِكْ

ساقَتْني إلى حَرَجٍ مَشْبوهْ

أضافَتْ أُمِّي واعِظَةً:

أَلْقي بَعيداً عَنْكِ هُمومَ الدُّنيا يا بِنْتي

وَارضِيْ بِالمَقْسومْ

مِنَ الأزواجِ أوْ الخَيْراتْ

كوني مِثْلَ بَقِيَّةِ خَلْقِ الله

دَعيني أَفْرَحُ في عُرْسِكْ

أمْنَحْكِ البَرَكاتْ

قُلْتُ لأُمِّي وَالعَيْنُ تُحاجِزُ دَمْعي

Mother, the voyages of my life

Have taken me to places west and east afar,

Beyond latitudes and longitudes,

Yet mother,

The letters of my stormy words are bubbling with my
    grief;

I am turned into a hurricane and a fiery flame

That blow into my very being.

The belying dreams transform my pulses,

Into a moaning tune and a broken flute.

Mother, my letters are a sail

That carries me into boisterous clouds.

Let my life be my witness:

I will never betray my rebellious spirit,

Or my aspiring voice

For a time yet to come.

I will never be reconciled with my lost days.

My skies will forever plant in the womb of my being

هِيَ الدُّنيا أفْلاكٌ ومَدارات

أخَذَتْني بَعيداً غَرْباً وشَرْقاً

خَلْفَ خُطوطِ الطُّولِ، خُطوطِ العَرْضِ

لَكِنِّي يا أُمِّي

حَرْفي يَحْتَرِقُ بِتِرْياقِ شُجوني

يُقَوْلِبُني إعْصاراً وشَرارا

يَجْتاحُ سُكوني

زِيْفُ الحُلْمِ يُحَوِّلُ نَبْضي صَوْتاً أوْ نايَاً مكْسورا

حَرْفي يا أُمَّاهْ شِراعْ

يُبْحِرُ في أنْواءِ غُيومي

فَلْتَشْهَدْ دُنيايَ بأنِّي

لَنْ أَتَخَلَّى عَنْ رَفْضي

عَنْ صَوتي الطَّامِحْ

في الزَّمَنِ الآتي

لَنْ أرْضى عَنْ زَمَني الضَّائِعْ

وسَتَبْقى سَمائي تَزْرَعُ في رَحْمِ كَياني

71

Shining moons

And glorious tidings in my desolate sphere,

So that I discern them star after star,

And reap from them a source of plenty for my verse

In order that I create better days in an unknown time.

Dhahran, January 1997

أقْماراً تَجْلوني

بِشارَةَ خَيْرٍ في بَيدائِيْ

أَسْتَجْلِيَها نَجْماً نَجْمَا

وَمَناهِلَ خَصْبٍ تَتَهَجَّى قافِيَتِي

حَتَّى يَتَخَلَّق يَوْماً زَمَنٌ آخَرْ

الظَّهران، كانون الثاني/يناير ١٩٩٧

Illusion

Because my eyes

Desirously flirt with yours;

Because my lips quiver

With the remnant of your muted muttering.

While my heart rejoices in your sins,

All my being trembles

And saddles its sigh,

In expectation of that

which buried deeply in blue memory.

March 8, 1999

تَعْليلٌ

لأنَّ عَيْنيَّ

تُغازِلانِ شَوْقَكَ

لأنَّ شَفَتَيَّ تَخْتَلِجانِ

بِثُمالَةِ تَمْتَمَةٍ لَمْ تَقُلْها

لأنَّ قَلْبي يَحْتَفي بِخَطاياكَ

تَرْتَعِدُ الجَوارِحُ كُلُّها

وتَسْرِجَ خُيولَ شَهْقَتِها

لِهذا الكامِنِ في مُتَرَدِّم التَّذكارِ

٨ آذار/مارس ١٩٩٩

I Shall Reconstruct the Speech

At the beginning of formation, space erupts

At the conclusion, the beginning turns into ruptures:

Is there a destination for a journey?

Is there a form for speech?

Save this whirling wind

That is enshrined in extinction!

What are the options of the ultimate direction?

Shadows are nothing but time,

Agonies enflamed by my steps

And the steps sip their scope from nightly wounds.

Am I heading for a dawn?

Perhaps!

Yet it is a night

سَأُعيدُ تَكْوينَ الكَلام

في أوَّلِ التَّكْوينِ يَنْبَجِسُ الفَضاءْ

في آخِرِ التَّكْوينِ تَتَفَطِرُ البِدايَهْ

هَلْ مِنْ مَكانٍ لِلسَّقَر!؟

هَلْ مِنْ كَلامٍ

غَيْرُ هَذي الرِّيحِ

تَأْتَزِرُ الفَناءْ

أيْنَ اتِّجاهاتُ النِّهايَهْ؟

الظِّلُّ أزْمِنَةٌ

تَباريحٌ تُؤَجِّجُها خُطاي

وَالخَطْوُ يَمْتَحُ مِن جِراحِ اللَّيْلِ فَرْسَخَهُ

أخْتارُ فَجْراً

رُبَّما!

لَكِنَّهُ لَيْلٌ

Whose steps groan in my dusk,

Diverting me from my love rhymes

Between hollow promises

Besieged by the confusion of the storytelling

Beware of my scream!

I will spread a handful

Of its glow

And touch the face of the planet

With ancient salt

I shall return to infinity

And unfold the galaxies

And cross paths with you, Gilgamish,

Whose name is engraved in my poems.

I will touch the flower which has long captivated the
    playwrights.

I shall reconstruct the speech

And shall re-arrange the story

خُطاهُ تَئِنُّ في غَسَقي

فَتَضيعُ قافِيَتي وَعِشْقي

ما بَيْنَ تَسْويفٍ وعودِ

تُحاصِرُها اضْطِراباتُ الرِّوايَةْ.

هِيَ صَرْخَتي

فَتَنَبَّهوا

فَأَنا سَأَنْثُرُ حَفْنَةً

مِنْ وَهْجِها

وَأَمِسُّ وَجْهَ الأَرْضِ

بالمِلْحِ القَديمْ

سَأَعودُ لِلأَمْداءِ

أَفْتَرِشُ السَّديمْ

وَأَمُرُّ بِكَ يا جِلْجامِشَ

المَنْحوتَ في شِعْري

وَبِزَهْرَةٍ فُتِنَ الرُّواةُ بها

سَأُعيدُ تَكْوينَ الكَلامْ

And restore for my suspended heart

Its pulsating life.

Between convulsions of fate

And reverberations;

Oscillate

The beginning and the end.

Dhahran, October 1995

وَأَعيدُ تَرْتيبَ الحِكايَهْ

وَأُعيدُ للقَلْبِ المُعَلَّقِ

خَفْقَهُ

بَيْنَ اخْتِلاجاتِ المَصيرْ

وَبَيْنَ جَلْجَلَةٍ

تُراوِدُها

البِدايَةُ وَالنِّهايَهْ

الظهران، تشرين الاول/اكتوبر ١٩٩٥

When the Moon Serenades

Suddenly, the moon shines

And lights my windows.

It beseeches me to touch its face,

To relax in a shadow of the horizon that extends

into intervals of my life,

Or to weave from its silvery light

a mantle for the shambles of my wilderness.

***

حَديثُ القَمَرِ

القَمَرُ الآنَ يُفاجِئُني
يَطُلُّ عَلى شُرُفاتي
يَسْألُني أَنْ أَتَلَمَّسَ في العَتْمَةِ وَجْهَهْ
أَنْ أَتَفَيَّأَ ظِلاًّ مِنْ أُفقٍ يَمْتَدُّ بِبَرْزَخِ عُمْري
أَوْ أَنْ أَنْسِجَ في فِضَّتِهِ
شَيئاً مِنْ أَشْلاءِ حَياتي

***

I serenade a moon that looms from beyond the mirrors of
     formation,
That makes my sight pierce into its all-encompassing
     cycle.
With a secret of my own,
The sadness of my spirit penetrates
Dunes that creep into the unknown.

* * *

أُحاوِرُ قَمَراً يَبْتَدي خَلْفَ مَرايا التَّكْوينِ

يُوغِلُ نَظَري في دَوْرَتِهِ الحافِلَةِ

بِــسِــيرٌ مِنْ ذاتي

تُوغِلُ أَحْزانُ الرُّوحِ

بِكُثْبانٍ تَرْحَفُ لِلْمَجهولِ

...

I step into the other phase.

The heat of the night rings a bell in my skull;

It shatters my mirror,

And demands that I journey into eras

Of the biography of my first memory.

No sooner I approach then it disappears.

* * *

أَدْخُلُ في أَرْوِقَةِ التَّشْريعِ الآخَرْ

حُمَّى الليْلِ تَدُقُّ بِرَأسي ناقوساً

يَنقُرُ مِرْآتي

لأُسافِرَ في حُقَبٍ وأَعْوامٍ

مِنْ سيرَةِ ذاتي الأُوْلى

ما أُدْرِكُها فَصْلاً يَأْتي لِيَزولْ

* * *

It is time fluctuating with its own vision,

Pilfering our blood,

With what it chews from the weeds of our lives,

Or with what we offer

Such as curly letters,

Or our melodies,

That we observe

After the storm, wrecked.

＊

هُوَ الزَّمَنُ المُتَقَلِّبُ في زَحْفِ رؤاهْ

فيما يَأخُذُهُ مِنْ حِبْرِ دِمانا

فيما يَمْضَغُهُ مِنْ عُشْبِ خُطانا

أوْ ما نُغْدِقُهُ إيّاهْ

تَجْعيدةُ حَرْفٍ

أوْ قافِيَةً

لِنَعودَ فَنَلْمَسُها

في وَجْهِ الريِّحِ حُطاماً ورُكاما

***

Oh, my diamond moon,

Beguiled in the prime of my life.

You, the light that shatters

The mirages of my path.

You, the ivory silence that follows me,

From the day of my birth

Till the flower on my grave.

Plant me in you

An unfading flower of time,

Or in your night a candle

Forever flickers.

***

يا قَمَري الماسيُّ
المُؤْتَنِسُ بِأخْضَرِ عُمْري
يا ضَوْءاً يَتَكَسَّرُ
فَوْقَ سَراب الطُّرُقات
يا صَمْتاً عاجِيّاً يُدْرِكُني
مِنْ شَهْوَة ميلادي
حَتَّى عُشْبَةِ قَبْري
ازْرَعْني في أعْطافِكَ
زهرة زَمَنٍ لا يَخْبو
أوْ في لَيْلِكَ قِنْديلاً لِلسَّهَر

***

Let me worship and pray.

Let me stay in the shrine of the night that is hidden in my
soul.

Let me devise for myself a language that chants

The psalms of a paradise yet to come.

Sharjah, UAE, April 1997

دَعْني أَتَبَتَّلُ وأُصَلِّي
أَتَهَجَّدُ في صَوْمَعَةِ الليْلِ المَخْبوءِ بــروحي
اشْتَقُّ لِنَفْسي لُغَةً تَهْمي
بِتَراتيلِ الفِرْدَوْسِ الآتي

الشارقة، نيسان/إبريل ١٩٩٧

Defeat

Had I been able to block

The sunshine

From entering my window,

I would not have been defeated by the nightingale

That perched on the remnant of my shoulder,

And implored me to be with him.

Dhahran, December 1993

هَزِيمَةٌ

لَوْ كانَ بِوُسْعِي

أنْ أَمْنَعَ أَشِعَّةَ الشَّمْسِ

مِنَ اخْتِراقِ زُجاجِ نافِذَتِي

لَما وَقَفْتُ مَهْزومةً أمامَ البُلْبُلِ

الذي حَطَّ عَلَى أَشْلاءِ كَتِفِي

وَناشَدَني الدُّخولَ مَعَهُ

في سِمْفونِيَّةِ التَّحْلِيقِ والغِناءْ

الظهران، كانون ألاول/ديسمبر ١٩٩٣

95

Seeking Forgiveness

I wept

For a stream of love whose source dried up,

For a firebrand that consumed itself,

For a widowed moon

That witnessed the senses flare.

I wept for the lotus tree of the soul

Whose fragrance penetrates the cycle of dryness.

I wept profusely

For each bleeding part

For a song that followed

The funeral of my lightning.

I wept long

غُفْرانُ دَمعي

بكَيْتُ

عَلى نَهْرٍ مِنَ العِشْقِ قَدْ جَفَّ نَبْعُهُ

عَلى جَمْرَةٍ أَيْقَنَتْ أَنَّها نَضَجَتْ

عَلى قَمَرٍ تَرَمَّلْ

بَعْدَ أَنْ شَهِدَ اشْتِعالَ الحَواسْ

بكَيْتُ عَلى سِدْرَةِ الرُّوحِ

عِطْرُها يَتَغَلْغَلُ في مَدارِ اليَباسْ

بكَيْتُ كَثيراً

عَلى كُلِّ نازِفَةٍ

مِنْ عُروقي

عَلى أُغْنِيَةٍ تُدْرِكُ

لَوْنَ انْطِفاءِ بُروقي

بكَيْتُ طَويلاً

Until I gave up seeking forgiveness from my tears.

Look at me,

Am I not the eyelid squeezing the grapevine!

Ottawa, January 5, 2000

فَما عُدْتُ أَنْشُدُ غُفْرانَ دَمْعي

هأنذا الجَفْنُ يَعْتَصِرُ الدَّاليَة

أوتاوا، ٥ كانون الثاني/يناير ٢٠٠٠

I Call You Not to Go

As a nymph exhaled from the clouds, I call you

From beyond the heavens,

I command you to exit from the shackles of time

So you can see God and the concealed;

To scribble a promise to the soul atop the minarets

And a supplication to paradise's Adam

And the celestial realm of the globe.

A nymph, I am!

Embrace my green spikelet,

And inhale my very breath,

And rest on the core of the soul and clay of creation

So you may see me,

And the rose may bud from the palms of the sand;

ما أَتَيْتُكَ كَيْ أَمْضِي

حوريَّةٌ أنا آتيكَ مِنْ زَفَراتِ السَّحابْ

مِنْ خَلْفِ السَّماوات

تَأَمُرُكَ أنْ تَخْرُجَ مِنْ تِمثالِ وَقْتِكْ

كَيْ تُبْصِرَ اللهَ والغَيْبَ

تَكْتُبَ فَوْقَ المَآذِنِ لِعِناقِ الرُّوْحِ عَهْداً

وَابْتِهالاً لآدَمَ الجنَّةِ

الأرْضِ وَالْمَلَكوت

حوريَّةٌ

فَعانِقِ سُنبُلَتي

وَازْفُرْ زَفْرَتي

وَأَسْتَرِحْ عَلى تَجاعيدِ الرُّوْحِ وَالطِّينْ

كَيْ تُبْصِرَني

وَحَتَّى تَطْلَعَ الوَرْدَةُ مِنْ نَخيلِ الرِّمالْ

And from the wings of the doves.

In my heart,

The unknown divine embraces you

From my parents' words, my soul comes unto you

So the branches of the child in me reach out to shade you.

From the conflagrations of your cave

The aura of light empowers my breast.

Between water and fire,

And between fire and water

And the rock

As a nymph,

My footprints strut in eternal soil.

I have not been united with you

So that I may depart.

My dreams are dedicated to the plight of the sun;

My prayers are to prophecies

That were made —

But never realized.

وَمِنْ أَكْمامِ اليَمامْ ها هنا

يَلْقاكَ الغُموضُ الإلهيُّ

تَأْتِيكَ الرُّوحُ مِنْ لُغَةِ أُميَّ وأَبي

كَيْما تُحاذي كَيانَكَ غُصونُ أطْفالي

مِنْ حَرائِق كَهْفِكَ

تَفيءُ بِفَضاءِ صَدْري المَسافاتُ

ما بَيْنَ الماءِ وَالنَّارْ

وَالنَّار وَالماء

وَالحَجَرْ.

تَرْفُلُ جُذورُ خَطْوي في التُرْبَةِ الأَبَديَّةِ

ما أَتَيْتُكَ

كَيْ أَمْضي

لِخُشوعِ الشَّمْسِ أحْلامي

وَصَلَواتي لِنُبوءاتِ العُهودِ

الَّتي جاءَتْ

ولَمْ تَأْتِ

Rejoicing

When your birds chirped,

Murmuring in my veins,

I celebrated my reticent voice,

And reticence rejoiced in me.

My heart belongs to your nebulous pulsation,

Let us escape to the tenderness under the skin,

While the world seems like blackened silver.

I implore you. Join me.

Dhahran, March 1994

احْتِفاءٌ

عِندَما أَنْشَدَتْني طُيورُكَ

تَحْتَ خَريرِ شَرايِيني

احْتَفَيْتُ بِصَوْتي

كَما احتَفى الصَّمْتُ بيْ

لِنَبْضِ غُيــومِكَ قَلْبي

إلى حُنُوِّ الوَريدِ نَفِرُ

وَالعالَمُ فَحْمٌ فِضِّيٌّ

وَقَدْ ناشَدْتُكَ أَنْ تَكونْ

الظهران، آذار/مارس ١٩٩٤

Awaiting

My wounds ooze bloody comets.

My fingers collect them

Awaiting

The day that will dawn for children

And transform my wounds into pearls

Whose nectar

Nurtures the horses of mercy

Which exist in the remoteness of human grief.

Dhahran, February 1994

نَزْفٌ

تَنْزِفُ الجِراحُ شُهُباً دَمَوِيَّةً
أُلَمْلِمُها عَلى أَصابِعي
إلى أَنْ يَأتي
فَجْرُ الأَطْفالِ
فَيُحَوِّلُها إلى لآلِئَ
تَتَغَذَّى عَلى رَحيقِها
جِيادُ الرَّحْمَةِ
في أَقاصي الأَنينِ البَشَري.

الظهران، شباط/فبراير ١٩٩٤

Final Rites

In the intimacy of my things rejoicing in desired chaos,

The breath of the space roars in the ribs of boredom,

Looking for a moment I aspire for certainty.

My sight roams,

My hands touch that that lurks in the fallacies of expectation,

To escape from the jungles of estrangement that gallop away
like words.

Yet I feel a greater mass of a wanton roaring,

The language that is bloodied by the wounds of its letters
does not assist me,

Nor the light of the day creep into the bustle of my veins,

As I divulge to time the untamed secrets that rave by the
curves of space,

From the emptiness of a death attacking me with logs of
reticence.

I witness the bursting of a light that crumbles at the temple
of night.

Beware!

طُقوسٌ أخيرةٌ

في حَميميَّةِ أشيائي المُلتذَّةِ بالتِماسِ فَوْضاها

تَسْري أنفاسُ المَكانِ مُزَمْجِرَةً في أضلُعِ الضَّجَرِ

بَحْثاً عَنْ لَحْظةٍ أتَدثَّرُ بِيَقينِها

تَجوبُ عَيْنايَ

تَلْمِسُ يَدايَ تُوَيْجاتِ هَذا الكامِنِ في ضَلالِ الاحتِمالاتِ

هَرَباً مِنْ أدغالِ غُرْبَةٍ تَبْتَلِعُ أحْلامَ لُغَتِنا

يَنْتابُني مَزيدٌ مِنَ الدَّوِيِّ الأرْعَنِ

لا اللُّغَةُ المُضَرَّجَةُ بِدِماءِ حُروفِها تُسْعِفُني

وَلا النَّهارُ يَدْنو مِنْ ضَجيجِ عُروقي

كَأنِّيَ أفْشي لِلْوَقْتِ بِجُموحِ أسرارٍ تَهذي بِانْحِناءِ "المَكانِ"

مِنَ قاعِ مَوْتٍ يُراشِقُني بِحَطَبِ الصَّمْتِ

أُتابِعُ انْبِثاقَ ضَوءٍ يَتَهشَّمُ في هَيْكَلِ اللَّيْلِ

فَلْتَحْذَري!

The hands of a moving clock speak to me.

Are we destined to be hung on a wall bursting with
   fancied existence?

I collect pieces of a sorrow that keeps haunting me.

I will not heed it.

I look at bodies dried by sheer density of nudity.

I trace its destructiveness creeping into the realm of a
   soul that was,

As if I taste the silence like a flute

To plant me a rose in Babylon.

Suddenly, life bursts in all that surrounds me.

Together, we whisper,

We reap from paradises of infinity,

To be enflamed as a glowing essence

Soaring in a galaxy of final rites.

Dhahran, January 1999

تَقولُ لي عَقاربُ ساعَةٍ تَمورُ

(أَحُكِمَ عَلَيْها أَمْ عَلَيْنا بِأَنْ نَتَعَلَّقَ عَلى حائطٍ زَمَنٍ يَتَفَجَّرُ بِأوْهامِ

وجودِنا!)

أَلَمْلِمُ دَثارَ زَفَراتٍ ما تَزالُ تُحَذِّرُني

لَنْ أَحْذَرَ!

هاأنذا أَشْهَدُ أَجْساداً أَيْبَسَتْها كَثافَةُ العَراءْ

أَقْتَفي خَرائبَها وَهْيَ تَتَسَلَّلُ إلى مَلَكوتِ الرُّوْحِ التي كانتْ

لَكأَنَّني أَحْتَسي الصَّمْتَ ناياً

يَزرَعُني فأُصارَ وَرْدَةً بابِليَّةً

يُبْعَثُ كُلُّ مَنْ حَوْلي

نُتَمْتِمُ مَعاً

نَمْتَحُ مِنْ فَراديسِ المَدى

نَشْتَعِلُ بَخوراً يُؤَجِّجُنا انْعِتاقاً

في شُموسٍ "طُقوسٍ أخيرَه

الظهران، كانون الثاني/يناير ١٩٩٩

My Love for You

My love for you is a creek of sadness.

My love for you is the mirth and birth of a bird,

Pronounced to you by a singing heart

While my sigh vibrates in my rib cage

A boxthorn, a broken sheath.

***

عِشْقي لَكَ

عِشْقي لَكَ نَهْرٌ مِنْ حُزْنٍ

عِشْقي لَكَ فَرَحٌ ووِلادَةُ عُصفورٍ

يُعْلِنُهُ صَهيلُ القَلْبِ عَلَيْكَ

واالآهَةُ في الأَضلُعِ

تَتَرَقْرَقُ كَالعَوْسَجِ أوْ كَالغَمْدِ المَكْسورْ

* * *

I submit my lulling whisper,

A crown for you to wear,

A nebula of stillness to take you inward.

From the momentum of my bleeding years,

I bring forth the sweetest of your memories,

The most precious of what you have lost;

A sonnet of rebellion is my love;

It invites you to sail into the unknown

Those yesterdays,

And the present, as the past advances toward death.

***

أُرْسِلُ هَدْهَدَتي

تاجاً تَلْبِسُهُ

فَيَسْكُنُكَ سَديمُ الصَّمْتِ

مِنْ هاجِسِ عُمْرٍ يَنْزِفُ

يَأْتيْكَ بِأَحْلى ما تَذْكُرْ

أَحْلى ما ضَيَّعْتْ

قَصيْدَةُ رَفْضٍ عِشْقي

تَدْعوكَ لأَنْ تُبْحِرَ في العُمْرِ اللامَرْئي

ذاكَ العُمْرُ السَّالِفُ

هَذا الحاضِرُ كَالماضي المُقْبِلِ في زَمَنِ المَوْتِ

* * *

We unite by the gleam of a twilight shore.

In Sufi rituals,

My love soars with transcendental wings:

Is it my weakness or my strength?

Is it hell or paradise?

Unsettled questions,

With burning answers

Enflamed by the scorch of the universe,

And the fury of the wind.

We unite as unborn secrets,

Yet its thirst lures our souls.

Lures and lures and lures . . .

Dhahran, May 1992

شاطِئُ ضَوْءٍ شَفَقِيٌّ يَجْمَعُنا

كَطُقوسٍ صوفِيَّةٍ

يُحَلِّقُ عِشْقي أَجْنِحَةً غَيْبِيَّةً

هُوَ شَىْءٌ مِنْ ضَعْفٍ أَوْ قُوَّهْ

نارٌ أَوْ فِرْدَوسٍ

أَسْئِلَةٌ لا تَهْدَأُ

وَإِجاباتٌ تَتَشظَّى

بِصَهْدِ الكَوْنِ

وعَصْفِ الرِّيْحِ

تَوَحَّدْنا كَمَجاهِلَ لا ميلادَ لَها

لَكِنَّ الرُّوحَ لَها تَظْمَأُ

تَظْمَأُ

تَظْمَأُ

الظهران، ايار/مايو ١٩٩٢

My Father's Tear*

You left a tear

Clinging to your eyelids

A Tear that will be a memory

That lasts forever

And whispers

The mystic secret

That stays with us

Perhaps this drop will divulge the secret!

Your vision retreated in despair,

Shrouded by concealed pain;

You closed your eyes and with one drop

You showed your encompassing love.

***

دَمْعَةُ داود *

وَتَرَكْتَ خَلْفَكَ دَمْعَةً
عَلِقَتْ بِأَهْداب الجُفونْ
أَبْقَيْتَها ذِكْرى لَنا
تَبْقى عَلى مَرِّ السِّنينْ
هَمَسَتْ بِعَيْنِكَ جُمْلَةً
تُنْبِينا عَنْ سِرٍّ دَفينْ
وَتَجولُ تَبْحَثُ بَيْنَنا
فَلَرُبَّما تَجِدُ اليَقينْ
فَارْتَدَّ طَرْفُكَ حائِراً
وَغَشاهُ مِنْ أَلَمٍ أَنينْ
أَغْمَضْتَهُ وَبِدَمْعَةٍ
أَوْجَزْتَ يا أَبَتِ الحَنينْ

* * *

In noble reticence you wondered

Why I was not beside you

And the words failed you

As your eyes lost the question;

The veil of death falling upon you.

Father, did you ask for me?

Or did you see me in your dream!

You rendered your soul peacefully

With one question lingering in your eye

Epitomized by a single tear,

A sad finale.

***

وَسَأَلْتَ في صَمْتٍ أَليمْ
وَصَمَتَّ يَعْوُزُكَ الكَلامْ
لِيَغيبَ في العَيْنِ السُّؤالْ
وَعَلَيْكَ قَدْ وَرَفَ الحِمامْ
أَسَأَلْتَ عَنِّي يا أَبي!
أَمْ جاءَ طَيْفي في مَنامْ!
أَسْلَمْتَ روحَكَ راضِياً
وَتَرَكْتَ في العَيْنِ السَّلامْ
لَخَّصْتَهُ في دَمْعَةٍ
تَبقى لِداودَ الخِتامْ

* * *

From distant seas, I came late

After your fate had been sealed,

After your graceful haughtiness had parted

And your voice was stifled

Your tears withered in your eyes;

Your sunrise darkened

Our one last meeting —

Not to be.

***

وَأَتَيْتُ مِنْ خَلْفِ البِحارْ

مِنْ بَعْدِ أَنْ وَقَعَ القَضاءْ

مِنْ بَعْدِ ما غارَ الشُّموخْ

مِنْ بَعْدِ ما بُحَّ النِّداءْ

مِنْ بَعْدِ أَنْ بَكَتِ العُيونْ

أَوْ جَفَّ في الدَّمْعِ البُكاءْ

مِنْ بَعْدِ أَنْ أَفَلَ الشُّروقْ

قَدْ عَزَّ يا أَبَتِ اللقاءْ

***

123

You, the most revered of men

Towered over us all

A shining star attracting our sight

In the darkness of the night.

You were the father

Who bestowed wholeness on our home

And raised a proud family.

A towering palm-tree

You will remain great among us

Unaffected by your demise.

***

قَدْ كُنْتَ يا شَيْخَ الرِّجالْ

طَوْداً عَلى هَذي السُّهولْ

نَجْماً تُطالِعُهُ العُيونْ

وَاللَّيْلُ في حَلَكٍ يَجولْ

وَبَقِيْتَ فينا والدَاً

تُضفي عَلى البَيْتِ الشُّمولْ

أَنْبَتَّ جيلاً سامِقاً

يَعْلو كَهاماتِ النَّخيلْ

سَتَظَلُّ فينا شامِخاً

هَيْهاتَ يُدْرِكُكَ الأُفولْ

* * *

125

What can I say to a father

Who dwells in my heart?

What can my eulogy say

With my lamenting soul!

Restraint is an eloquent narrator

But a crushing pain

My throbbing heart floods with tears,

Weeps in grief.

But of all these tears

There is one, only one

I will remember forever.

***

ماذا أَقولُ لِوالِدٍ!

وَهْوَ في قَلبي يُقيمْ

ماذا تَقولُ قَصائِدي

وَالشِّعْرُ مَحزونٌ كَليمْ

فَالصَّمْتُ أَبْلَغُ مُخْبِرٍ

لَكِنَّهْ وَقْعٌ أَليمْ

يَبْكي فُؤادي لَوْعَةً

وَالدَّمْعُ مُنْهَمِلٌ سَديمْ

سَأَظَلُّ أَذْكُرُ دَمْعَةً

تُبْقيكَ في قَلْبي حَميمْ

آثَرْتَ رَحْلاً بَعْدَها

وَرَضيتَ جَنَّاتِ النَّعيمْ

* * *

Your blessed grave will remain

Forever a monument in *Makkah*

Beside the holy *Kaaba* of Allah,

Resting in the bliss of its shadow

Embracing its holy earth

With blowing musk

You have accepted the calling of God

With the serenity of meditative prayers;

A true believer all your life you have been

Waiting for this true day.

Now, you rest in peace . . .

While from above, your soul graces ours.

***

تَبْقى بِمَكَّةَ شاهِداً

يا والِدي نِعْمَ الضَّريحْ

جاوَرْتَ كَعْبَةَ رَبِّنا

كَيْما بِظِلِّهِ تَسْتَريحْ

وَمَكَثْتَ تَلْثُمُ تُرْبَها

وَالمِسْكُ مِنْ ضَوْعٍ يَفوحْ

لَبَّيْتَ دَعْوَةَ خالِقٍ

بِدُعاء مُبْتَهِلٍ صَريحْ

أَوْقَفْتَ عُمْرَكَ مُؤْمِناً

تُعْلي لِمَوْعِدِهِ الصُّروحْ

وَالآنَ تَمْكُثُ آمِناً

وَعَلَيْنا مِنْ فَوْقٍ تَلوحْ

* * *

Yet it is an exhortation

If I am shocked by your death

And have learned its lesson

Death is a drink

Whose cup goes round.

Your memory, Dawood,

Is a treasured ritual.

A drop on your eye remains

Purer than the purest gold;

An agony,

An intimate bond.

Jeddah, 24 April 2000

---

*   On the last sight, when my father was in his grave, a single teardrop was seen hanging on his eyelid. Some explained it as pain and agony by which he expressed the absence of one of his children. I was the only one not present at his deathbed.

    This poem was inspired by reflecting on that single teardrop, and was written later, after the funeral had taken place before I had arrived in Jeddah from Canada.

المَوْتُ حَقٌّ واجبٌ

لَكِنَّهُ عِظَةُ النُّفُوسْ

فَلَئِنْ فُجِعْتُ بِمَوْتِهِ

وَعَلِمْتُ ما مَعْنى الدُّروسْ

إنَّ المَنِيَّةَ شُرْبَةٌ

وَتَدورُ في الدُّنيا الكُؤوسْ

ذِكْراكَ داودُ لَنا

يا والِدي أَحْلى طُقوسْ

تَبْقى بِعَيْنَيْكَ دَمْعَةً

أَنْقى مِنَ التِّبْرِ النَفيسْ

تَبْقى بِقَلْبي حَسْرَةً

لَكِنَّها ذِكْرٌ أَنيسْ

جدة، ٢٤ نيسان/ابريل ٢٠٠٠

* فارق والدي، الشيخ داود الحياة وبعينيه دمعة كانت آخر ما شوهد على جفنه وهو يوارى في التراب، وقد فُسِّرت بأنَّها تعبير عن حزن وألم على أحد أبنائـه أو بناته لم يره حوله وهو على فراش الموت. وقد شاءت الاقدار ان اكون غائبة حين وقوع الحدث الجلل. وكانت لي بمثابة الدمعة التي عبَّر فيها والدي يرحمه الله عن غيابي وعتابه لعدم رؤيتي حوله.

ومن وحي تلك الدمعة، كانت قصيدتي: "دمعة داود" وفاء لوالدٍ وذكرى ستظلُّ معي.

I Have Hoisted My Sail

I have hoisted my sail

To triumph over the tempest

And to face unpredictable gales;

The quest of the unknown

Will inscribe my destiny

Never again will I fear ghost or ghoul.

With zealous steps, I press forward;

I will never dread those gory thorns,

Nor shy away from a battle

Though teeming with phobia and death

I will preserve my life.

***

إنِّي قَرَّرْتُ الإبْحارَ

أطْلَقْتُ شِراعي
لِيُغالِبَ عَصفَ الرِّيحِ المَجبولَ
بِأَسْئِلَةِ الأنْواءِ المَجْهولَه
لُغَةُ اسْتِمطارِ الآتي
تَكْتُبُني
إيقاعُ المَجهولِ يُهادِنُني
لَنْ أخْشى شَبَحاً أو غُولا
يُورِقُ خَطْوي
أتَقَدَّمْ
لَنْ يَخْذُلَني شَوكٌ يُدْميني
لَنْ أُحْجِمَ عَنْ مَعْرَكَةٍ
فيها الهَوْلُ وفيها المَوْتْ
ما دامَتْ مَعْرَكَتي تُحْييني

***

133

With these oars of mine

I'll start the journey

Over the seas

To find my direction

There, beyond the unfathomable depths,

Beyond the stretches of the night,

Which are lured by my verse,

The shadows of the trees looming in my eyes,

And the fruits of Paradise,

The inner songs will be calling:

Why be scared!

Your compass lies in you.

And the flute of my stillness resonates:

Don't hesitate;

Be guided by your faith!

Jeddah – Dhahran 1978

هَذا مِجْذافي أُطْلِقُهُ

لِمَحارِ الْكَوْنِ

هُناكَ وَراءَ البُعْدِ اللامَرْئي

وَخَلْفَ تُخومِ الليْلِ

الْمَسْكونِ بِقافِيَتي

تَلوحُ لِعَيْني

أَعْنابُ الفِرْدَوْسِ

ظِلالُ الأشْجارْ

إيقاعُ المَجْهولِ يُكاشِفُ حُنْجُرَتي:

"فيمَ الخَوْفُ

وَأَنْتِ تُجيدينَ الغَوْصِ!"

وَتُرَدِّدُ قيثارَةُ صَمْتي:

"ولِمَ الخَوْفُ!"

يُعاوِدُني صَمْتي:

فَلِمَ الخَوْفُ!

ما دامَتْ ثِقَتي بَوْصَلَتي

هِيَ كُلُّ يَقيني

جدة – الظهران، ١٩٧٨